WORLD'S BEST
ILLUSIONS

 W9-BOO-600

A COMPENDIUM OF ILLUSIONS

Bend your mind!

Prepare to scratch your head and rub your eyes in disbelief. This book is full of brain-boggling optical illusions.

An optical illusion plays tricks on your eyes and brain. Are you seeing what your eyes see or what your brain thinks it's seeing? Optical illusions work in different ways. Some are based on how your eyes work and how light falls. And some are based on what your brain expects to see, rather than what's really there. Let the brain-bending begin ...

Smile, please! Or maybe these pictures don't show two smiling faces? Turn the book upside down to find out.

Look hard, really hard, to see the shadowy figures in the banister.

2

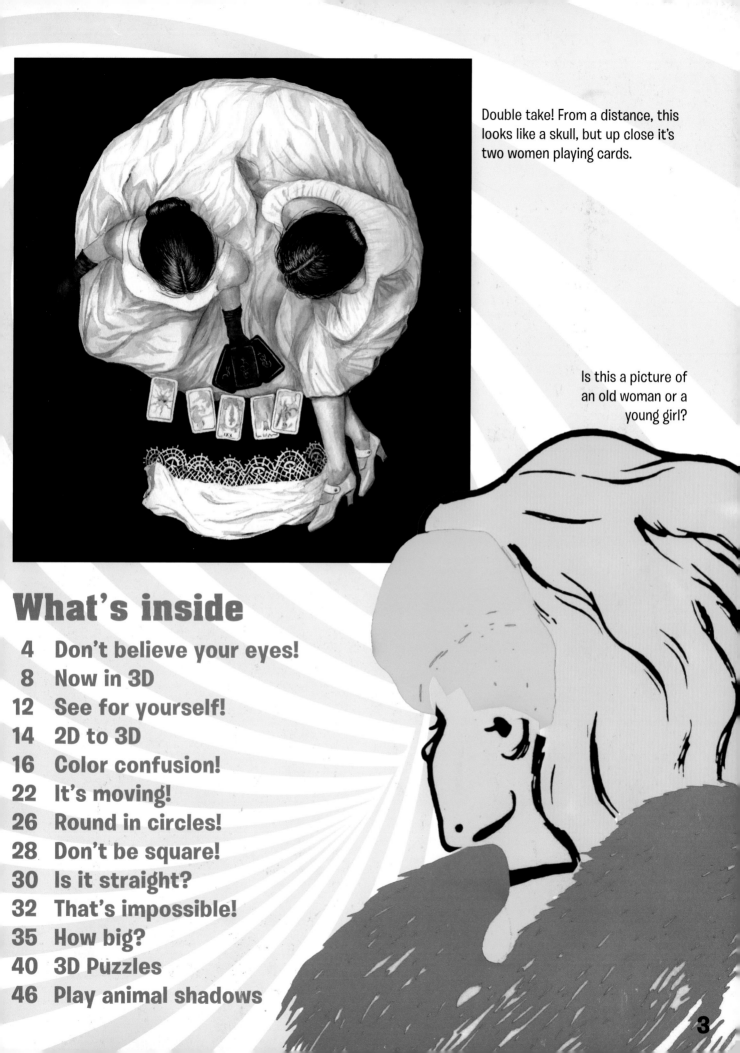

Double take! From a distance, this looks like a skull, but up close it's two women playing cards.

Is this a picture of an old woman or a young girl?

What's inside

3

Don't believe your eyes!

Watch out! You can't always trust what you see. The illusions on this page play tricks based on what you expect to see rather than what is there. Is there a hole in the middle of the woman? Or is she holding up a mirror? From experience, usually, you can tell if things are far away or near using perspective, but not here.

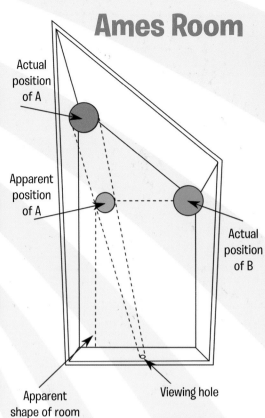

Actual position of A

Apparent position of A

Actual position of B

Apparent shape of room

Viewing hole

Yikes! What's up? When you look through the peephole into this Ames room, you assume the room is square, but really the ceiling slopes steeply. This makes the children appear giant and tiny.

The small scale of the palace below is perplexing, too. It looks big and small at the same time.

Is that real?

Got you! These paintings look real but they aren't. Photographic detail helps make a flat wall or floor look like a real 3d scene. These hyper-realistic paintings are called trompe l'oeil, which means 'trick of the eye' in French.

Now in 3D

Put on your 3D glasses. Look at the picture of the baseball player. To understand why it looks 3D, you need to understand how we see. Most humans have binocular vision, which means they have two eyes, see things in 3D and can judge distance.

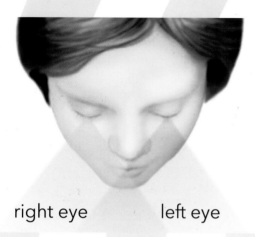

right eye   left eye

Usually, our eyes are about 2-3 inches apart, so each eye sees an object from a slightly different viewpoint. The brain joins the two views together to make a 3D picture.

Test your binocular vision. Hold your thumb up at arms-length then close one eye. Now try closing the other eye. As you switch between each open eye, your thumb should 'jump' backward and forward against the background.

Two Pictures

Put on your 3D glasses. Look at the way these two pictures combine to make one 3D image of New York.

1. Close one eye and look at this picture through the red lens only. Does the red picture fade away?

2. Now close the other eye and look through the blue lens. Does the blue picture fade away into nothing?

3. Now turn the book round to see what happens when the two pictures are combined. Look at the picture through your 3D glasses with both eyes open.

3D

See for yourself!

Eyes to Brain, come in, please! The eyes send messages to the brain, but sometimes the messages are confusing and the brain gets out of step. Test out these experiments for yourself. Show your friends, too.

MONEY FROM NOTHING

Place two large coins between your index fingers. Rub the coins together with quick up-and-down strokes. Watch closely. Can you see a third coin between the original two coins? Kaching!

HOLE IN THE HAND

This won't hurt! Hold a small tube up to your right eye. Now, with your palm facing you, place your left hand against the side of the tube. With both eyes, look into the distance. Can you see a hole that has mysteriously appeared in your hand?

A FINGER SAUSAGE

Really? Yes, point your index fingers towards each other until they touch. Then slowly bring your hands up to about 8 inches in front of your nose, then look at where the fingers touch. Now draw your fingers slightly apart and look through the gap. Focus on something in the distance. Can you see a floating sausage has magically appeared in front of your eyes?

GLASS BALL

Which way is up? When light travels through glass, it can change direction, or refract. This glass ball has made the image behind look upside down.

BENT SPOON

Is the spoon broken? No, the water is bending the light that is bouncing off the spoon so it just looks broken.

REVERSE STRIPES

Light plays all kinds of tricks. This glass acts almost like a magnifying glass. The stripes seem to bend towards the center.

2D to 3D

OK, it's time to concentrate and trick your brain into thinking a 2D pattern is a 3D picture with these optical illusions, called autostereograms. Usually, when you look at a page, both eyes see almost the same thing so the brain presumes the image is flat. When you look at an autostereogram, the brain is tricked into thinking both eyes see the same thing, but really the 2D pictures are slightly different. The brain jumps to the conclusion that the picture is 3D.

How to view an autostereogram

The aim is to make the image seem to float above the background.

First, concentrate at a point in the middle of the 2D picture. Relax your eyes. Rather than look at the picture, look through and beyond it. The picture might appear slightly out of focus. Once you notice the 3D image, it will become easier. Try not to refocus on the 2D picture because you will lose the 3D picture. Keep on practicing.

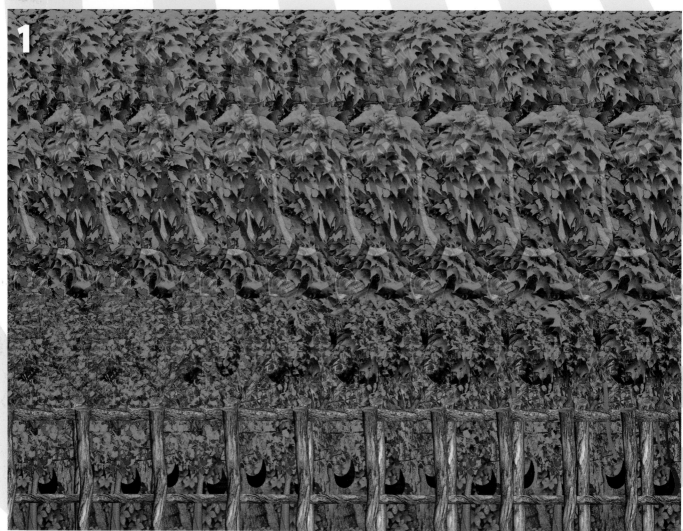

1

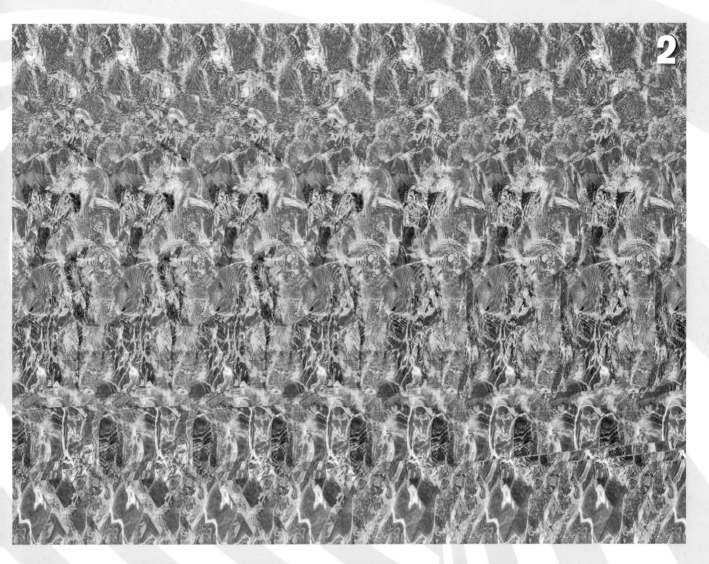

Chess set

This autostereogram shows 3D images, rather than flat 2D patterns. When you look beyond the picture, can you see all the chess pieces on the board in 3D?

Color confusion!

Red is red and blue is blue! Well, yes, but you can't always trust your eyes when it comes to color. Why does a leaf look green? In nature, you see color as a type of light that bounces off a surface. The different colors that make up light reflect off surfaces. But it's not all about light. Your brain is also busy considering other factors, such as the colors nearby and whether there are shadows. Illusions can make you doubt your own color-crazy eyes.

Has this woman got one blue eye and one grey eye? No, the blue eye looks blue only because of the pink background. Really both eyes are grey.

Does the middle bar go from light to dark? No, it's the same shade. The graduated background makes it just look as if it goes from light to dark.

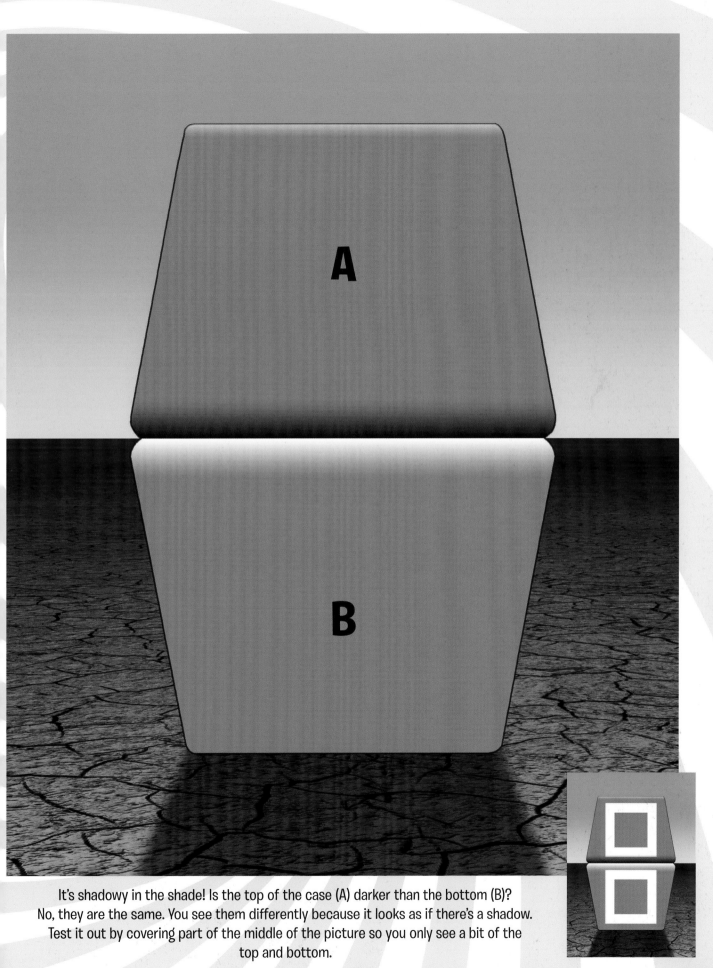

It's shadowy in the shade! Is the top of the case (A) darker than the bottom (B)? No, they are the same. You see them differently because it looks as if there's a shadow. Test it out by covering part of the middle of the picture so you only see a bit of the top and bottom.

Hard to believe, but these hearts are the same color!
They appear to be different colors because of the colors nearby.

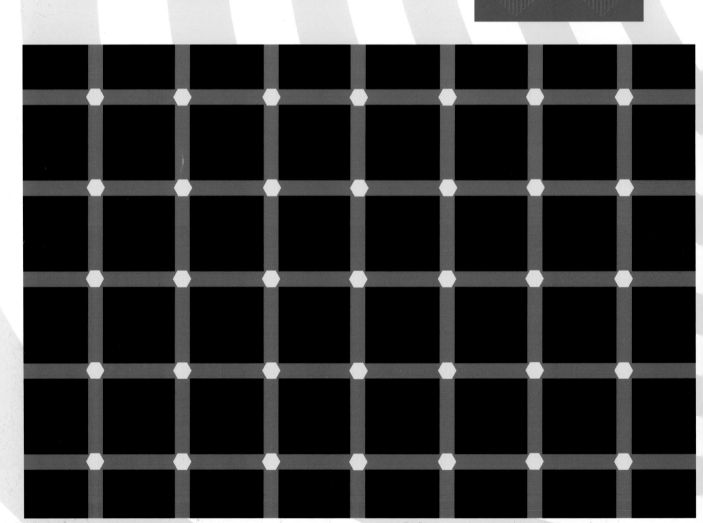

These dots are all yellow. When you scan across the grid, they appear to change color to green.

Which stegosaurus is darker? Aggh! They are both the same. The background colors help to make them look lighter and darker.

Which is lighter, square A or B? Surprisingly they are both the same. Your brain takes account of the shadows and thinks B is lighter.

A

B

It looks as if this cat has eyes of different colors, but they are both grey.

Are these dogs different colors? Look at the picture opposite to see that really they are both the same color.

Are the tiles in the middle of the top side and the middle of the left side different colors? No, they are the same. The shadows make them appear different.

It's moving!

Wow! Can you see patterns swirling in front of your eyes? These are called motion illusions. The patterns confuse your eyes and brain so much, the pictures appear to move. Try looking at the patterns with your peripheral vision (out of the corner of your eyes). The swirling light and dark patterns also confuse your brain by triggering 'motion detector cells'. Your brain knows something is moving but gets it wrong. It thinks the patterns are moving, but really it's your eyes.

Round in circles!

Is this a cone or a tunnel?

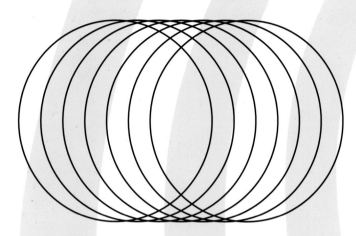

Flip-flop images can appear to change direction.
Is the front of this tube on the right or left?

Go for a spin! To make the wheels on the bicycle
turn, move the page counter-clockwise ↺.

26

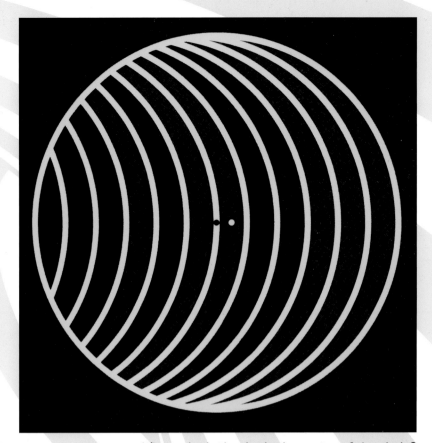

These two spirals look identical, but one is made from one line the other from two. Can you work out which is which?

What color is the dot in the center of the circle? Is it yellow or black?

Can you see a spiral pattern? Look again. Really, it's many circles.

Make your head spin! Are the shorter lines straight or bent? Place a ruler on any straight edge to find out.

Don't be square!

Is the long beam at an angle to the block beneath? Surprise! The beam and block are parallel or the same distance apart.

What do you see? You decide. A large cube and a small cube? A large cube with a corner missing? Or a cube in the corner of a room?

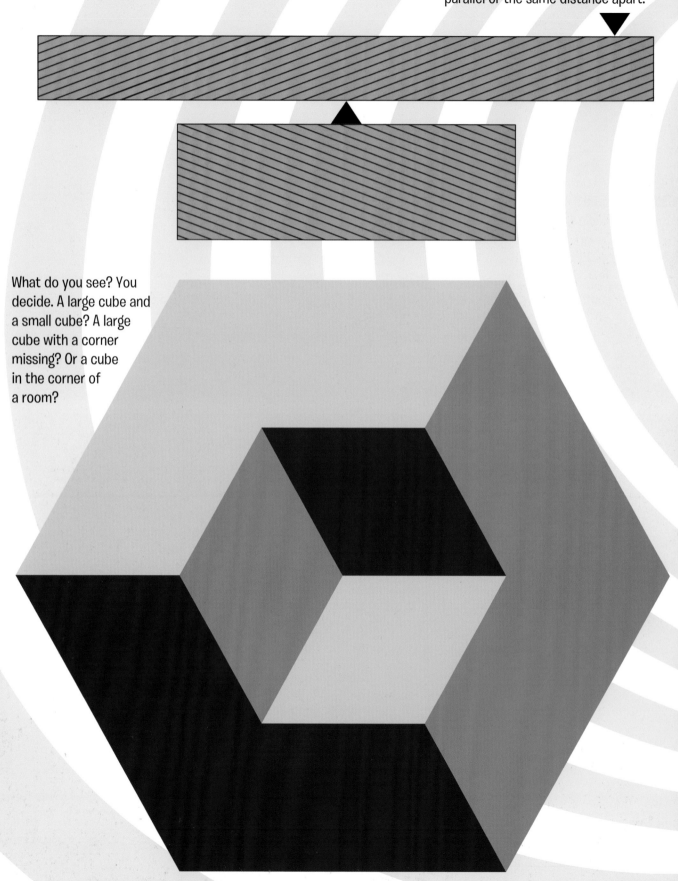

Look at this group of squares.
Can you see mysterious grey spots appearing
between the blue boxes?

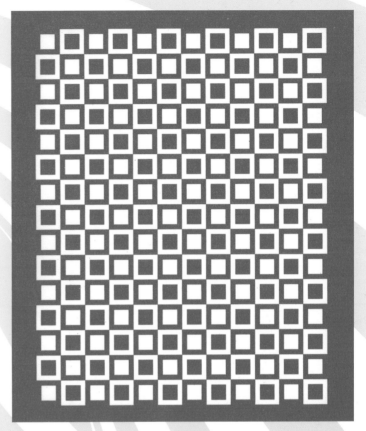

This pattern looks wobbly and topsy-turvy.
Now look again at eye level. It's neat and straight.

How many cubes can
you see in this picture?
It depends on how you look!
For one answer, can you
find six cubes?
For another answer, can you
find seven cubes?

Are the sides of the square
inside the circles bent?
Check them out
with a ruler.

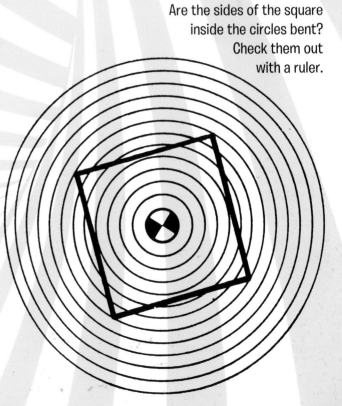

Is it straight?

Get ready to bamboozle your brain with LINES. These pictures are called distortion illusions. Straight lines look bendy, short lines look long, and the opposite, too. Puzzling perspective, pattern and background help to confuse your brain so you misjudge what you are seeing.

How strange! These four planks appear bent but really they are straight and true!

Are the long slanting lines parallel, or an equal distance apart? Not sure? Measure with a ruler to find out.

Are the stripes inside the circles completely horizontal? Yes, they just seem to slope towards the center.

Which line on the left lines up with the single line on the right? It's tricky! Use a ruler to find out.

Are these towers leaning at the same angle? Measure them to see if you are right.

Are these tiles straight or wonky? They are all straight.
Check by placing a ruler along the orange lines.

That's impossible!

Imagine walking along the edges of each of these structures. Are you walking up or down? Is the path never-ending or does it break? In the pictures, unusual perspectives, or angles of vision, play tricks on your eyes. The impossible seems possible.

How long till you reach the top of these stairs?

The top of the window looks as if it doesn't meet at the top, but it does. The pillar in front creates an illusion.

Weird! It's almost as if you can see this face front-on and from the side.

How big?

Wise up to sizing up! It can be difficult to judge the size of an object. When your brain tries to judge if an object is big or small, it takes into account the object's surroundings. It asks, are the objects nearby bigger or smaller? Also, it knows that things usually look bigger close-up. But an unusual perspective can play clever tricks. Sometimes, the brain gets it wrong.

Tunnel Vision

Which woman is taller? Both women are the same height.
Your brain is confused by what's near and what's far away.

Who's bigger?

Is the wizard bigger than the magician? Or maybe the magician is taller than the wizard? Measure each one to find out.

Pen puzzle

Which pen is longer? Are you sure? Check them out!

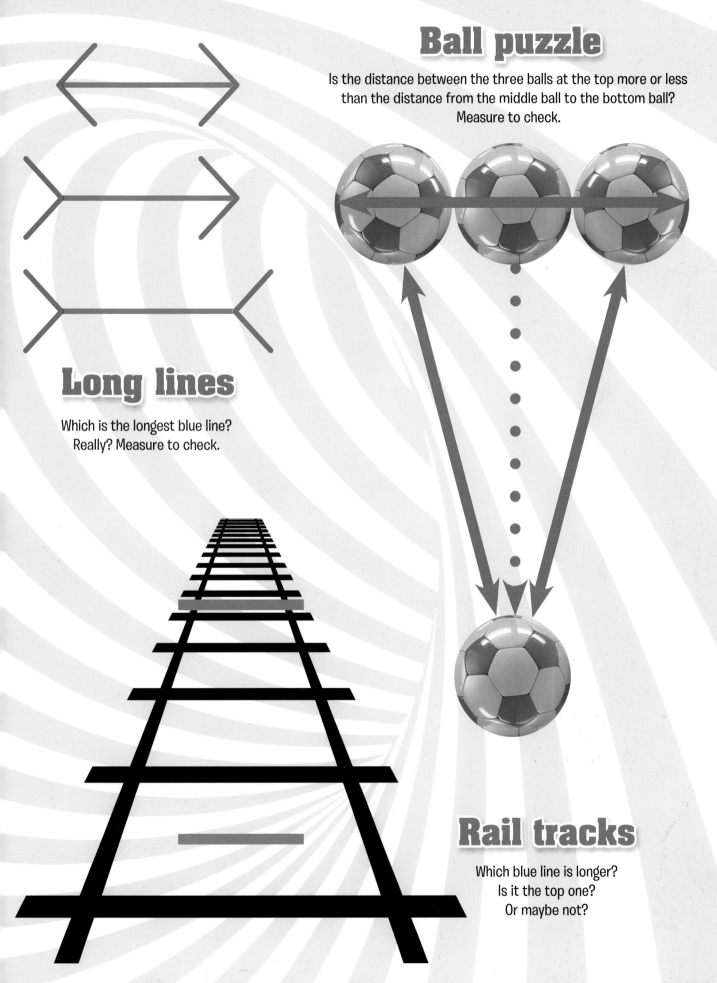

Ball puzzle

Is the distance between the three balls at the top more or less than the distance from the middle ball to the bottom ball? Measure to check.

Long lines

Which is the longest blue line?
Really? Measure to check.

Rail tracks

Which blue line is longer?
Is it the top one?
Or maybe not?

Table top

Is the yellow table bigger than the orange table? Or is the orange table bigger than the yellow table? In fact, the surface area is the same. The different shapes of the tables and the odd perspective make it confusing.

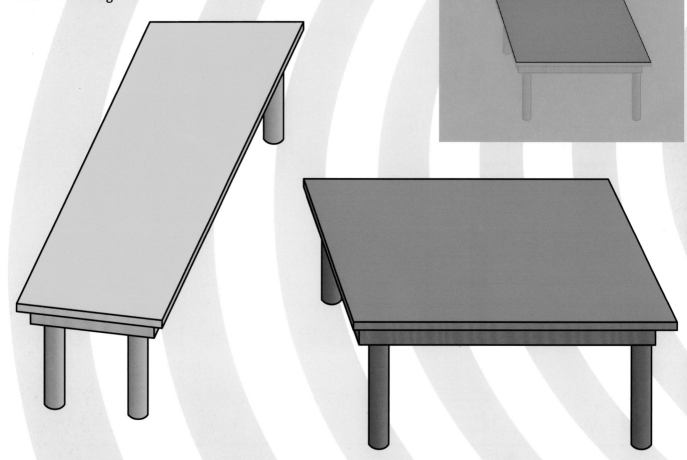

Which distance is greater?

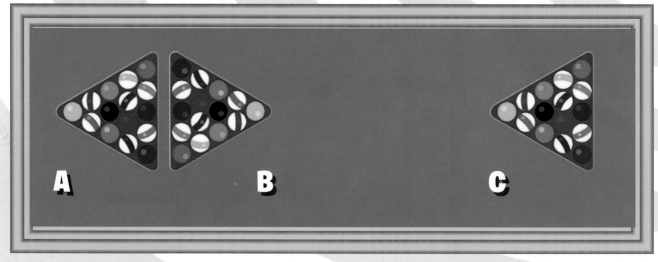

Which distance greater - A to B or B to C? Use a ruler to find out!

Who is taller?

Not sure? The figures are the same height. The parallel lines confuse your sense of perspective and what is near and what is far away.

Which star is bigger?

Don't be fooled! Both stars are the same size. The red circles confuse your brain.

3D Puzzles

Put on your 3D glasses to see these images jump off the page. How does it work? Two pictures - one in red and one in blue - are printed overlapping. When you look at the pictures through your 3D glasses, you see in stereoscope vision, which means the images are superimposed on top of each other. Woah! The picture leaps off the page.

3D hidden objects

The boxes on the right don't look very interesting! Put on your 3D glasses to see hidden objects magically lift off the page.

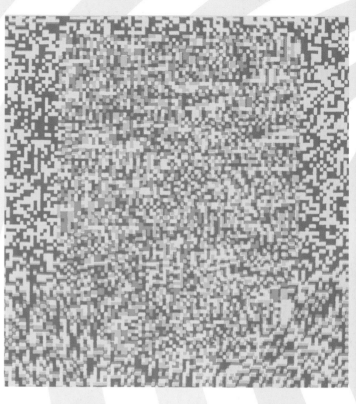

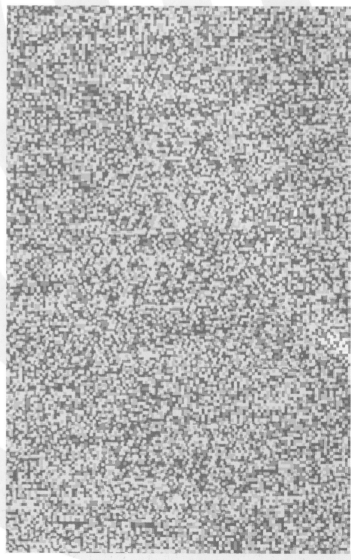

Is this the top edge of a building or the corner of a room?

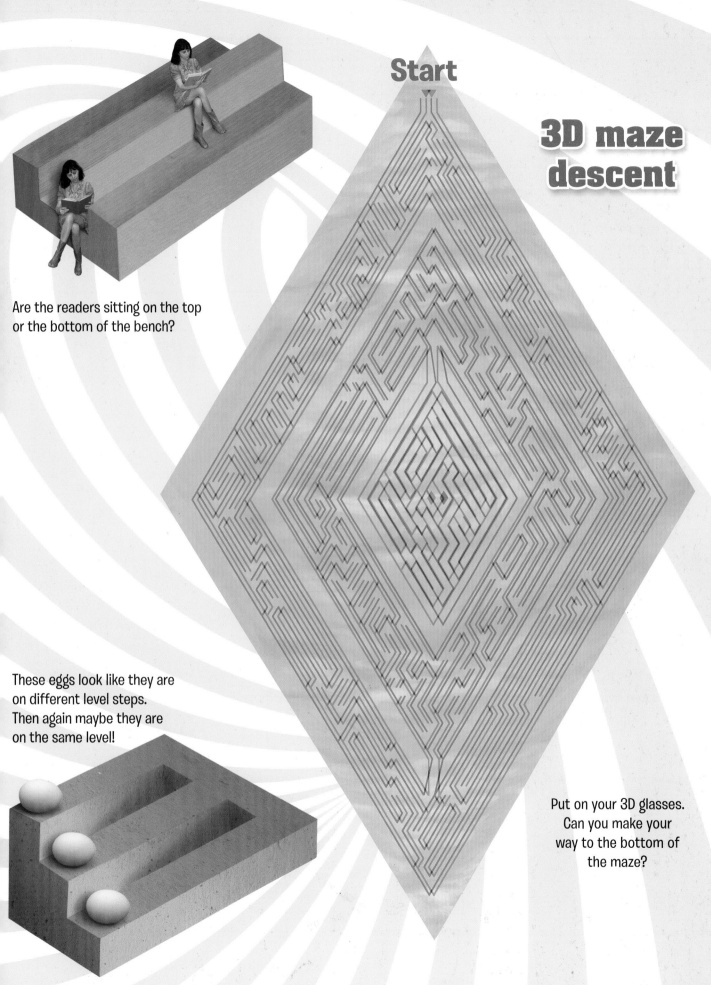

3D maze descent

Are the readers sitting on the top or the bottom of the bench?

These eggs look like they are on different level steps. Then again maybe they are on the same level!

Put on your 3D glasses. Can you make your way to the bottom of the maze?

Tangled Kites

Put on your 3D glasses. Which number string belongs to which kite?

station

Wearing your glasses, which number route leads to the station?

Crossed Phone Lines

A B C D E F G H I J K L

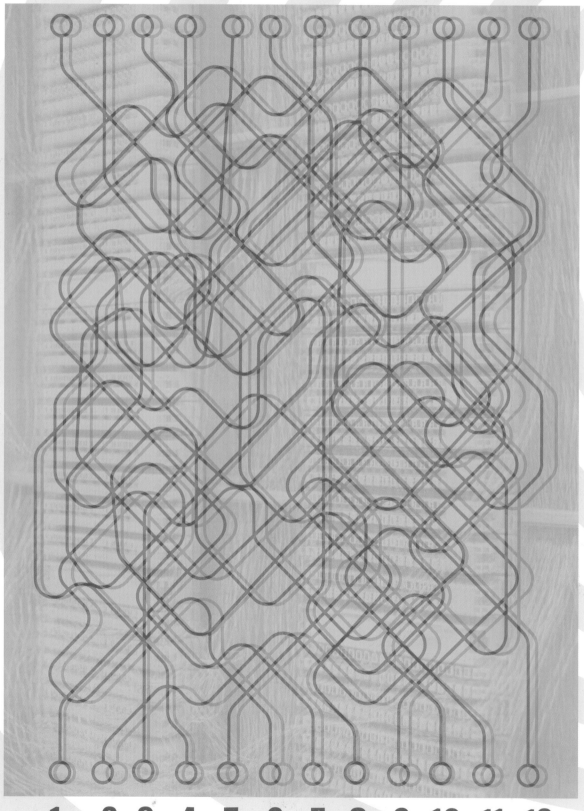

1 2 3 4 5 6 7 8 9 10 11 12

Put on your 3D glasses. Can you unravel these phone lines? Each letter is connected to a number.

Crystal Ball Quest

Look through your 3D glasses to see the floating steps leading to the crystal ball.
From the top of the page, which steps will you take to reach the ball?

Play animal shadows

It's showtime! Create animal shadow puppets with your friends.
All you need is a bright light, a blank wall, and your hands!

Alligator

To make the alligator's jaws snap, pull and push your hands apart and together quickly, but don't move your fingers.

Kangaroo

To make the kangaroo jump, tip the right hand backward and forwards quickly. At the same time, move both hands across the wall.

Dog

To make the dog prick up his ears, first lower one thumb then raise the other.

Pig

To make the pig's tail curl and uncurl, bend and straighten the little finger on the left hand.

Elephant

Pick up a pretend peanut with the two middle fingers of your left hand, which make the trunk. Move the nut to the elephant's mouth.

Horse

To make the horse gallop, raise and lower your hands, moving them forwards across the wall.

Woodpecker

To make the woodpecker dart for an insect, move your hands forward quickly, then bring them back again.

Moose

To create a moose on the loose, keep your hands in the position shown then toss them backward slightly.

Tortoise

To make the tortoise move her head very slowly, move the first two fingers of your left hand.

Rabbit

To make the rabbit scratch her nose, use your right forefinger, which is one of the paws. Make the ears wriggle by moving the last three fingers on your left hand.

Goose

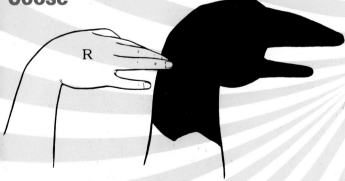

Open and close the goose's beak by moving your fingers up and down. Every now and then, dip your hands down to make the goose stoop to gobble up a grain of corn.

Snail

To make the snail appear to slither forwards, move both hands very slowly across the wall. To move the horns, bend your fingers on your right hand.